Latino Americans and Religion

Hispanic Americans: Major Minority

Latino Americans and Religion

Frank DePietro

Mason Crest

Mason Crest
370 Reed Road
Broomall, Pennsylvania 19008
www.masoncrest.com

Printed and bound in the United States of America.

First printing
9 8 7 6 5 4 3 2 1

Library of Congress Cataloging-in-Publication Data

DePietro, Frank.
 Latino Americans and religion / by Frank DePietro.
    p. cm.
 ISBN 978-1-4222-2322-2 (hardcover) — ISBN 978-1-4222-2315-4 (series hardcover) — ISBN
 978-1-4222-9326-3 (ebook)
 1. Hispanic American Catholics—Religious life. 2. Hispanic Americans—Religion. I. Title.
 BX1407.H55D47 2012
 200.98—dc23
                            2012010651

Produced by Harding House Publishing Services, Inc.
www.hardinghousepages.com
Interior design by Micaela Sanna.
Cover design by Torque Advertising + Design.
Printed in USA.

Contents

Introduction

by José E. Limón, Ph.D.

Even before there was a United States, Hispanics were present in what would become this country. Beginning in the sixteenth century, Spanish explorers traversed North America, and their explorations encouraged settlement as early as the sixteenth century in what is now northern New Mexico and Florida, and as late as the mid-eighteenth century in what is now southern Texas and California.

Later, in the nineteenth century, following Spain's gradual withdrawal from the New World, Mexico in particular established its own distinctive presence in what is now the southwestern part of the United States, a presence reinforced in the first half of the twentieth century by substantial immigration from that country. At the close of the nineteenth century, the U.S. war with Spain brought Cuba and Puerto Rico into an interactive relationship with the United States, the latter in a special political and economic affiliation with the United States even as American power influenced the course of almost every other Latin American country.

The books in this series remind us of these historical origins, even as each explores the present reality of different Hispanic groups. Some of these books explore the contemporary social origins—what social scientists call the "push" factors—behind the accelerating Hispanic immigration to America: political instability, economic underdevelopment and crisis, environmental degradation, impoverished or wholly absent educational systems, and other circumstances contribute to many Latin Americans deciding they will be better off in the United States.

And, for the most part, they will be. The vast majority come to work and work very hard, in order to earn better wages than they would back home. They fill significant labor needs in the U.S. economy and contribute to the economy through lower consumer prices and sales taxes.

When they leave their home countries, many immigrants may initially fear that they are leaving behind vital and important aspects of their home cultures: the Spanish language, kinship ties, food, music, folklore, and the arts. But as these books also make clear, culture is a fluid thing, and these native cultures are not only brought to America, they are also replenished in the United States in fascinating and novel ways. These books further suggest to us that Hispanic groups enhance American culture as a whole.

Our country—especially the young, future leaders who will read these books—can only benefit by the fair and full knowledge these authors provide about the socio-historical origins and contemporary cultural manifestations of America's Hispanic heritage.

chapter 1
Ancestors

Luis is a quiet young man. He doesn't talk a lot. But he could tell some stories. He's had his share of problems.

Luis grew up in California. His neighborhood was poor. People didn't have jobs. He started selling drugs and ended up in jail.

But Luis got a second chance at life. He met a **chaplain** in jail. The chaplain told Luis that God loved him. He had a good plan for his life. Luis trusted him.

When Luis got out, he joined a church. That was a good choice for him. Now Luis spends time each week volunteering. He hands out food to people who need it. Luis smiles when he talks about how grateful he is to be helping others.

Luis changed his life because of his beliefs. He found strength in Christianity. He's like millions of other Latinos who also think religion is important.

Of course not all Latinos are alike. Religion is part of many of Latinos' lives. But not everyone's. Each person is different.

There are lots of Latinos in the United States. Most of them are Catholic. That's a type of Christianity. Others are Pentecostal. That's another kind of Christianity. Some Cubans follow Santería, a religion with African roots. A few are Muslim, Jewish, or they believe in another religion.

> A **chaplain** is a church leader who works in a jail, on a ship, in a hospital, with the Army, or in another place outside of a regular church.

LATIN AMERICA

There are lots of countries to the south of the United States. Most people who live in those countries speak Spanish. Some of them speak Portuguese or English. All together, all of those countries are called Latin America.

Latinos are people who come from any Latin American country. They could speak Spanish. Then we can also call them Hispanic. Or they could speak Portuguese. Or English. Or even French. Those people aren't Hispanic. But they are Latino because they live in Latin America.

Some Basic Geography

The American continents are big. They include North and South America. They also include Central America.

North America is where the United States is. To our north is Canada. To our south is Mexico. Mexico is part of Latin America.

South of North America is a piece of land called Central America. There are a few small countries here. They are also part of Latin America. Further south is South America. There are more Latin American countries here.

There is one more part of Latin America. Many small islands lie to the south of the United States. They are in the Caribbean Sea. Many of those islands are considered part of Latin America.

LATINO AMERICANS AND RELIGION

Map showing much of Latin America

Aztec gods

 # Native Religions

Before Europeans came to the Americas, lots of people lived here. There were at least 40 million people in North, South, and Central America.

There were lots of different **cultures** and languages. There were also lots of different religions.

The Aztecs were one large group. They lived in southern Mexico and Central America. The Aztecs built up a big empire. They were powerful.

The Aztecs had their own religion. They built huge pyramids and made beautiful art as part of their beliefs.

The sun and moon, stars, and corn were all Spirit Beings who ruled nature. Each thing had a spirit. Each one was a god.

The Aztecs had feast days to celebrate their religion. They also had religious **ceremonies**. One sort of ceremony was the **sacrifice**.

The sun god needed energy to keep rising and setting. The Aztecs believed they had to sacrifice human beings to give the sun god energy. Each year, thousands of sacrifices were made. Today people don't understand how the Aztecs could kill so many people.

Cultures *are ways that groups of people look at the world. Customs, language, religion, celebrations, and beliefs are all parts of a culture.*

Ceremonies *are a series of actions done to celebrate something with spiritual meaning.*

A **sacrifice** *is when an animal or person is killed as a gift to God or the gods.*

Europeans

Soon, **native** people wouldn't be the only ones in America. The Europeans were coming. And they brought a new religion with them.

For a long time, native groups were the only people in the Americas. Europeans stayed on their side of the globe. People on one continent didn't even know the other continent existed.

That all changed. Europeans built better ships and started sailing farther and farther. They eventually found the Americas.

Spain was the main country that sent explorers to the New World. That's what they called the Americas. For the people in Europe, the land that lay on the other side of the Atlantic Ocean seemed like a new world. For the people who lived there, of course, it wasn't new at all. It was just the world.

The King and Queen of Spain were Catholics. Catholicism is a very old form of Christianity. Religion can do a lot of good for the world. But it can also be used to do bad things. The King and Queen used it to start wars. They used it to hurt people.

In Spain, they wanted everyone to practice Catholicism. They hunted down people who believed in other religions. This was called the Spanish Inquisition. Then people had to **convert**. Or they would be killed.

The Spanish brought these ideas with them. They wanted all the Natives they met to be Catholics. They thought the Native's religions were wrong.

A **native** is someone who was born in a particular place. If you were born in Hawaii, for example, you are a native of Hawaii. We also use the word "Native" to talk about the people whose ancestors have lived in the Americas since long before white people came here. People also call these groups of people Indians— but they're not from India at all!

To **convert** means to change the way you believe.

The landing of Columbus

Christopher Columbus

Everyone knows that Columbus landed in the Americas in 1492. He first set foot on the island of Hispañola in the Caribbean Sea.

A group of Arawak Indians watched from the shore. They saw the strange white men step on shore. They didn't know what to think.

They probably weren't thinking that Columbus and his men were going to try to change their religion. Or that he would want to make them slaves.

Columbus was a Catholic. He believed that God had saved his life years before. His ship had been blown up when he was still on it. But he sur-

LATINO AMERICANS AND RELIGION

vived. There must have been a reason, he thought. He believed God had a special job for him to do.

Columbus thought he was supposed to bring Catholicism to people who didn't have it. He believed that was why he had survived the accident. And that's what he did. He started a way of acting that all the European explorers would follow: forcing Natives to become Catholic.

The Conquistadors

The conquistadors (that's a Spanish word for "conquerors") were Spanish explorers. They came to the Americas to take over. They too were Catholic.

Hernando Cortés was a conquistador who landed in Mexico. First he met with the Aztecs there. They took him up to the top of the highest pyramid.

On top, Cortés saw the signs of human sacrifice. He was disgusted. So he shoved a statue of the sun god down the steps. In its place, he put a Catholic Virgin Mary and a cross.

The Aztec priests were angry. How dare he place this tiny woman and her baby in place of the sun god? But they didn't want to go to war. They had seen the Spaniards' weapons. So they let it go for now.

Hernando Cortés

Other conquistadors had the same beliefs. They thought their religion was right. They were sure the Natives were wrong. They didn't treat the Natives' religion with respect.

Change

Right away, Europeans tried to convert the natives. They also killed them. And made them into slaves. And took their lands. It's not surprising that most people didn't want to convert. Why would they want to believe in a religion that showed them so much hatred?

But today, most Latin Americans are Christians. Something changed their minds. There were two main reasons why people ended up converting to Christianity.

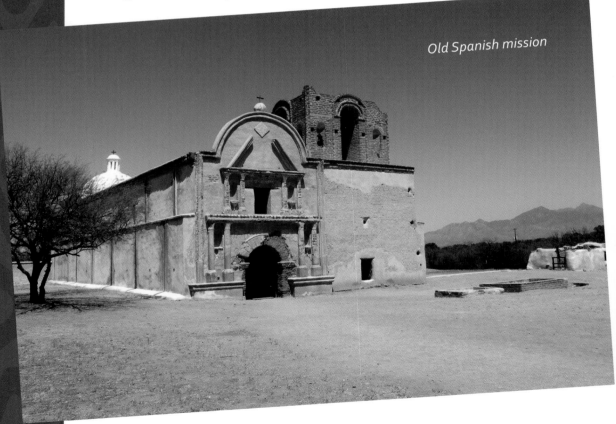

Old Spanish mission

LATINO AMERICANS AND RELIGION

One was the Virgin of Guadalupe. Her story convinced a lot of Latinos to become Catholic. We'll tell that story in Chapter 3.

The other reason that people converted were European friars. Friars were Catholic men who served God by helping others.

Many friars came to the Americas. They wanted to convert people too. But they didn't use violence to do it. They used words and good acts.

One friar preached a sermon that shocked his Spanish listeners. He told them they were not good Christians. No one who treated the Natives the way they did was really following the teachings of Christ. His listeners didn't like that. They threatened to hurt him.

Other friars supported Natives too. Bartolomé de Las Casas was one of them. In 1514, he was a chaplain for some conquistadors in Cuba. He watched in horror as the conquistadors killed people.

Watching that changed Las Casas forever. He used to own Native slaves. Now he let them go. He started talking to people about the Natives' rights.

No one listened to him in Cuba. So he went back to Spain. There he talked to the government about how badly the Natives were treated. He got a law passed that protected them. But no one really followed it.

People say that there are two sides to the Church in the Americas. One was cruel. It had to do with the conquistadors and gold and slaves. The other side had to do with helping the poor and working for peace.

Spanish Missions

Spanish people kept on trying to convert natives for hundreds of years. In the 1700s, they moved up to what is now the United States. A man named Friar Junípero Serra was chosen as their leader.

The Spanish set up missions in North America. The missions had a lot going on. There were churches there. There were gardens and animals.

From the missions, Serra and others converted people. Serra managed to **baptize** more than 6,000 natives in California.

They did this mostly with peaceful ways. They talked to people. They tried to make Christianity make sense to them. They knew they couldn't force people to just change their religion.

Other Faiths

Most Latin Americans today are Christian. But some follow a different religion. There are a few thousand Latino Muslims. Some have converted recently. Others have been Muslims for generations.

Spaniards made some African Muslims slaves. They shipped them to the New World. Islam traveled to Latin America. So Islam has been in Latin America for a long time.

Some Latinos have recently become Muslims. They see it as returning to their roots. It's a way of honoring history.

Buddhism is another growing religion with Latinos. Buddhism comes from Asia. It encourages **meditation** as a way of finding peace. It's a now a religion for people all over the world.

Some Latinos are Jewish. During the 1800s, many Jews came to Argentina, Chile, Uruguay, and Mexico. Their **descendants** still practice Judaism. Some moved to the United States and brought their religion with them.

To **baptize** *means to dip someone in water as a sign that they have decided to become a follower of Jesus Christ. It's a Christian ceremony.*

Meditation *is a relaxation technique that involves emptying the mind of thoughts.*

Descendants *are children, grandchildren, great-grandchildren, great-great-grandchildren—and so on.*

HISPANIC OR LATINO?

In the 1980s, the U.S. government came up with the name "Hispanic" for people who speak Spanish and live in the United States. Not everyone likes this name. Many people don't like the way the term lumps everyone together based only on language. The people in North and South America who speak Spanish have a very different culture from Spain's. Other people use the word "Latino" for this same group of people. They like this word better because it has more to do with Latin America than with Spain.

The fact that Hispanics—or Latinos—don't agree on which term to use for themselves shows how different they all are. They come from many different countries. They have different stories. But at the same time, Hispanic American cultures have many things in common. They share many of the same stories. They often worship God the same way. Many of the same things are important to them. They are proud of their art and music. They celebrate the same holidays.

chapter 2
The Catholic Church

Catholics all share some things in common. They all believe in God. They believe that Jesus is the son of God they believe that by following the Church's rules, people can go to heaven. They also believe in the Virgin Mary and other saints. They believe in the Bible. They go to **mass**.

But Latino Catholics add their own flavor to Catholicism. They have their own religious history. So they make the religion their own.

> **Mass** *is a service where Catholics eat a little bit of bread and wine. The bread and wine are symbols of Jesus Christ's death. It's a way to remember the life and death of Jesus.*

 ## A Living Faith

Millions of Latinos could share memories of their parents' faith. Most went to Catholic Church when they were young. Even if they don't go now, their parents and grandparents did.

In the United States, most Hispanic Americans continue practicing Catholicism. Almost half of all Catholics are Latinos. That's a big deal for the Church. All over the United States, Catholic churches are changing how they do things. They want to welcome Latinos. Latinos also have their own Catholic churches.

Sometimes there are too many Catholics for the number of priests. There are thousands of worshippers for each priest. He has to do a lot of work! There's a need for more priests. Especially Latino priests.

Serving so many people is hard. But many priests like that they get to see so many people.

But the priests can't do it all themselves. They rely on ordinary people to help them. Many church leaders are not part of the **clergy**. They have other jobs. They just help out when they can. They teach religious classes. They visit sick people. They read the Bible in church.

 ## Creativity

Latino Catholics share many things with other Catholics. But they also have their own **traditions**.

> **Clergy** *are people who are official leaders in the church.*
>
> **Traditions** *are ways of doing things that people have practiced for many years.*

Father Lorenzo Miranda, priest at a Catholic church in La Puente, California

Latino masses tend to be creative. They don't look like every other mass. The **congregation** sings special songs. Members honor certain saints, depending on the church.

Worship is livelier. Most non-Latino masses tend to be more serious. But in Latino-masses, people play the guitar and clap their hands. It's more like a party.

Latino Catholic traditions might look a little different too. On Good Friday, Christians around the world remember Jesus. In the United States, people gather quietly in churches to listen to sad speeches about the death of Jesus. It's a time for thinking and quiet.

For Latinos, Good Friday is a celebration. They take to the streets. They parade, carrying a figure of Jesus down the road. They also think about the death of Jesus, but in a very different way.

Mural at Dolores Mission in Los Angeles

Sometimes the leaders of the Catholic Church don't know what to do with Latinos. The way they practice Catholicism is different from what other people do. Sometimes the Church wants them to tone down the festivities. But mostly they realize that it's just a different way to practice the same religion. They're glad that Hispanics are so excited about their faith.

The Poor

Many Latinos in the United States are poor. It's hard to find good jobs. It's hard for them to keep jobs. Learning English can be tough. This is especially true for recent **immigrants**. It's also true for people who didn't get here legally.

Latinos work hard to follow Jesus' teachings about helping others. Many Hispanic volunteers run programs to help other people. They feed the poor. Or they care for people who are sick. Or they help young people get out of gangs. There's a lot a church can do.

One church in Santa Ana, California, set up a food warehouse. They got grocery stores to give them food. The church fed hundreds of people every week. But so many more people were hungry.

The church set up something called the Kingdom **Coalition**. Sixty different churches belong to it.

A hand-carved image of Christ provides a focal point for worship in a Latino church.

Immigrants *are people who leave their home countries to move to another country to live.*

A **coalition** *is a group of smaller groups, all working together for the same goals.*

SANTOS (SAINTS)

The Catholic Church teaches that the Saints in heaven have a special closeness to God. Latino Catholics feel especially close to Los Santos (the Saints). People who have struggled with problems in life can especially relate to the Saints who went through the same things. The Saints were human beings, just like all of us. But they won out over their struggles. And now Catholics believe they help us win too. The Virgin Mary, the Queen of Heaven, is above all Saints.

Latin Saints

LATINO AMERICANS AND RELIGION

Together, they help many, many people. They give them food, education, and other things.

FAITH AND FAMILY

More than any group in the United States, Latinos are known for the way they value "familia" (family). Latino homes often have a married couple with kids, plus others like grandparents or cousins. Religion is an important part of Latino families. Practicing religion at home is important too. In Central America, religious classes and Bible studies take place in family settings. Many Latino homes have spaces set aside for family altars. These altars might include paintings or small statues of Christ or the saints. Candles are burned before the home altar, and families join together in prayer.

chapter 3
Our Lady of Guadalupe

Remember the Virgin of Guadalupe from Chapter 1? She was a main reason that natives converted to Catholicism

Now, *Nuestra Señora de Guadalupe* (Our Lady of Guadalupe) is everywhere in Mexico and the United States. She's in a few other countries too. Her image is on everything. You can find her on the walls of stores and homes. She's on posters and **shrines**. She's even on things like air-fresheners!

Our Lady usually is wearing a blue cape. Her skin is very tan. She looks downward, smiling. Her hands are folded and she looks like she's praying.

Even if a Mexican isn't Christian, he or she usually still believes in the Virgin of Guadalupe. Otherwise, they might not be counted as Mexicans!

> *A **shrine** is a place where people worship. It's usually a fairly small place.*

 **The Story**

One day in 1531, a man named Juan Diego was out walking to Mexico City. The conquistadors had come to his land a few years before. He had been through a lot of changes in his life.

Juan Diego was Christian, but he was also a Native from the group called the Aztecs. He walked by an Aztec shrine for the mother goddess. She was very important to the Aztecs. Then suddenly, he saw the Virgin Mary. She was right in front of him, shining with light.

The Virgin Mary had dark skin. She looked Aztec. She spoke in the Aztec language. But she was definitely the Virgin Mary. She told Juan that she was the mother of God. She said that everyone should believe in her. It didn't matter if they were Aztec or European.

Juan was amazed. He went and found a **bishop** in Mexico City. The bishop didn't believe him. He told Juan he would need a sign in order to believe him.

> *A **bishop** is an important leader in the Catholic Church.*

Soon after, Juan saw the Virgin Mary again. She told him to take off his cape and fill it with flowers. He did that. Then he took the cape to the bishop. He shook the flowers out of the cape. A picture of the Virgin Mary was left behind on the cape.

Now the bishop believed him. So did lots of other people.

They build a big church for Mary in Mexico City. That's where Juan first saw her. Many, many people come to the shrine even today. They think of Mary as the Virgin of Guadalupe. She belongs to them in a special way. The cape that is on display is supposed to be Juan Diego's original cape.

The Virgin of Guadalupe convinced many people in Latin America to become Catholic. If she could appear to an Aztec, then she could appear to anyone. Christianity wasn't just a white man's religion.

Image of the Virgin Mary

LATINO AMERICANS AND RELIGION

Bronze relief of Juan Diego

WHERE DID THE NAME GUADALUPE COME FROM?

The name Guadalupe had important meanings both for Indians and Spaniards. Speaking in the Aztec language, the Virgin told Juan Diego her name was Coatlaxopeuh. That is pronounced "quatla-soo-pay." Coatlaxopeuh means "One who crushes the snake." It sounds similar to the Spanish word Guadalupe.

For Spanish speakers, the name Quatlasupe reminded them of the Virgin of Guadalupe in their homeland. Our Lady of Guadalupe is the name of a famous statue of Mary that stands in Spain. During the Middle Ages, people came from all over Spain to pray to the Virgin of Guadalupe. Christopher Columbus, Hernando Cortés, and Bishop Zumarraga all worshiped at her chapel before traveling to the New World. So they changed the New World Virgin's name to "Guadalupe."

Inspiration *is a word for new ideas and new strength.*

 ## An Inspiration

Our Lady of Guadalupe gives people **inspiration**. Latinos feel like she is their mother. She helps people heal when they get hurt. She helps people calm down when they're angry. She helps people get through bad luck.

Virgin Mary of Guadalupe painting

A street mural in Los Angeles reflects the Native traditions woven through the Virgin's story.

Lots of people have stories about how Our Lady helped them. They claim they recovered from being sick after they prayed to her. Or that they suddenly found money. Or that their children got well after having a terrible illness.

It's hard for other people to believe their stories sometimes. But the people who tell them believe them. That's what counts.

Women love her especially. In some Latino communities, women don't have a lot of power. They aren't equal to men. But they look to Our Lady for comfort.

The Virgin of Guadalupe is an example of a powerful woman. Men and women alike worship her. So why can't other women be powerful too? She has helped women believe that they can have a bigger role in their community.

Guadalupe is also important for workers. Latinos often face hard times at work. They have to deal with low pay. And **discrimination**. People treat them badly because they're Latino.

But they know they can count on Our Lady. They pray to her to make things better. She's part of Latinos' everyday lives.

> **Discrimination** *is unfair treatment because a person is different in some way from the larger group.*

A modern mural of the Virgin of Guadalupe

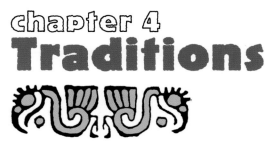

chapter 4
Traditions

There is a story that some Latinos tell. According to the story, a Mexican man tried to cross the United States border around thirty years ago.

He crossed the desert by himself. He got lost and hungry. The border patrol caught him. He tried again and again to get across. One day, he met a young man who offered to help him.

This time, with his helper, the man was successful. He reached the United States. He wanted to pay his helper, but he didn't have any money.

The guide told him that he could repay him later. He could come back to a town in Mexico and ask for Señor Romo.

Years later, the Mexican man went back. He went to the town and asked for Señor Romo. No one seemed to know him. At last, an old woman showed him a picture. It was the guide!

"That's impossible," said the woman. "This is a young priest who died in 1928. That was a long time ago." She took the man to a church to show him the priest's bones.

Since then, Señor Romo has become a saint. The Pope named him a saint in 1990. People trying to cross the border pray to him. They want him to help them like he helped the first immigrant.

Folk Religion

Latino beliefs are filled with "folk traditions." These are traditions that come from people's everyday experiences. They weren't learned from books. They weren't taught in class or by the Church.

ILLEGAL IMMIGRATION

Getting to the United States legally can be hard. Legal immigrants have things called visas or green cards. Without one of those, you can't legally come to the United States to live. Visas and green cards are hard to get. But some people really want to come here. So they come illegally.

They don't bother to wait years and years for a green card. They need to come now. Maybe they need to make money for family back home. Or their families already live in the United States. Or they're not safe in their homes for some reason.

People who immigrate illegally to the United States have to really want to come. They have to cross a desert and brave the immigration officials. It's dangerous. People die. Or they get caught and sent back. Then they try all over again.

The United States government tries to keep illegal immigrants from coming here at all. Over the years, the United States has passed more and more laws to do that.

The Border Patrol is in charge of keeping illegal immigrants out. It uses fences and walls along the border. It uses checkpoints where cars have to stop before they can drive across the border into the United

States. Members of the patrol go up and down the border, guarding it.

Patrol agents use helicopters. They use high-tech equipment like motion-sensors. The whole point is to catch illegal immigrants before they get across.

But despite all that, there are still probably about 11 million illegal immigrants in the United States. There could be as many as 20 million! A lot of them come from Latin America. And a lot of those come from Mexico.

The Catholic Church accepts some folk beliefs. The Virgin of Guadalupe is one. But it doesn't approve of other folk beliefs. They're too different than **traditional** Catholicism.

Latino Catholics believe in a lot of Saints that belong especially to Latin America. For example, Mexicans pray to Saint Romo. Other Latinos pray to other Saints.

Cubans worship Saint Lazaro (Lazarus). The put pictures of him on walls. He is a thin man, leaning on crutches. His picture usually includes two dogs.

> **Traditional** *has to do with the way things have always been done.*

Lazarus was a poor man that is mentioned in the Bible. He begged for food from a rich man. But the rich man didn't help him. Both Lazarus and the rich man died. After death, the rich man suffered because he wasn't a good man in life. Lazarus was a good man. He went straight to heaven.

People who face poverty and unfairness pray to Saint Lazarus. They think he'll understand their problems.

 Folk Art

Latinos create art to show their religion. Folk art is more than just a painting or a statue. It's a **symbol** of faith.

> A **symbol** is something that stands for something else. It has a deeper meaning.

Hispanic people use pictures of the Virgin of Guadalupe and others all the time. They put them up to remind them to be strong. They want to be good people. Pictures of Saints remind them to be good.

Pictures also tell stories. For example, Cubans pray to a different picture of the Virgin Mary. They pray to Our Lady the Virgin of Charity. In pictures, she wears a gold dress, holding Jesus. Beneath her feet are three sailors in a canoe, in the middle of a storm. One sailor is black. One is white. The other is a mix of black and white. The picture tells a story. It tells about how three men on a boat in a storm found a statue of the Virgin Mary when they were lost at sea. It was dry, even though it should have been wet. After they found the statue, they found their way safely to shore. It was a miracle that showed that God was with them.

The picture also tells another story. It says that people of all colors should work together. It doesn't matter if we're black or white or both. All of us are the same before God.

 Celebrations

Each Saint has a special day. They are called feast days. And each feast day is a party. Different Hispanic people celebrate different feast days.

December 12 is the Virgin of Guadalupe's feast day. That is the most important one in a lot of Latin American countries. Catholic churches celebrate all over the Americas. There is lots of eating. There is praying. There's music and dancing.